Backyard Animals
Beavers

Blaine Wiseman

www.av2books.com

MEDIA ENHANCED BOOKS
AV² BY WEIGL
ADDED VALUE • AUDIO VISUAL

BOOK CODE

E 7 7 6 1 6 6

AV² by Weigl brings you media enhanced books that support active learning.

AV² provides enriched content that supplements and complements this book. Weigl's AV² books strive to create inspired learning and engage young minds for a total learning experience.

Go to **www.av2books.com**, and enter this book's unique code. You will have access to video, audio, web links, quizzes, a slide show, and activities.

Audio
Listen to sections of the book read aloud.

Video
Watch informative video clips.

Web Link
Find research sites and play interactive games.

Try This!
Complete activities and hands-on experiments.

Due to the dynamic nature of the Internet, some of the URLs and activities provided as part of AV² by Weigl may have changed or ceased to exist. AV² by Weigl accepts no responsibility for any such changes. All media enhanced books are regularly monitored to update addresses and sites in a timely manner. Contact AV² by Weigl at 1-866-649-3445 or av2books@weigl.com with any questions, comments, or feedback.

Published by AV² by Weigl
350 5th Avenue, 59th Floor
New York, NY 10118
Website: www.av2books.com   www.weigl.com

Library of Congress Cataloging-in-Publication Data

Wiseman, Blaine.
  Beavers / Blaine Wiseman.
      p. cm. -- (Backyard animals)
  Includes bibliographical references and index.
  ISBN 978-1-60596-877-3 (hard cover : alk. paper) -- ISBN 978-1-60596-879-7 (soft cover : alk. paper) --
  ISBN 978-1-60596-880-3 (e-book : alk. paper)
  1. Beavers--Juvenile literature. I. Title.
  QL737.R632W57 2010
  599.37--dc22
                                    2009050474

Printed in the United States of America in North Mankato, Minnesota
1 2 3 4 5 6 7 8 9 0 14 13 12 11 10

042010

WEP264000

Editor Heather C. Hudak   **Design** Terry Paulhus

Photo Credits
Weigl acknowledges Getty Images as its primary photo supplier for this title.

Contents

Meet the Beaver

Beavers are **mammals** that belong to the **rodent** family. They live near streams, rivers, lakes, and marshes all over North America. The only places beavers do not live are the very northern parts of Canada and parts of Florida, Nevada, and California. Beavers also can be found in Europe and Asia.

Beavers are known for their long, sharp teeth. They cut down trees with their teeth and use the sticks and logs to build **dams**. This floods the land around the dam, making a perfect home for these water-loving rodents.

These large rodents live in family groups called colonies. Most beaver colonies are made up of a mother, father, and their children.

A beaver can swim up to 5 miles (8 kilometers) per hour.

It takes two beavers working together about 15 minutes to cut through a 4-inch (10-centimeter) tree branch.

All about Beavers

There are two **species** of beaver. One species lives in North America, while the other lives in Europe and Asia. Both species look very much alike. For example, they have thick fur and long front teeth. Both Eurasian and North American beavers have a fat body with short legs. This makes them move slowly and clumsily on land.

Underwater, beavers are graceful swimmers. They have a long, flattened tail that helps them swim. Beavers have waterproof fur that keeps their skin dry. It also helps them swim faster.

Beavers have flaps of skin in their ears and nose. These flaps close when they swim, keeping out water.

Sizes of Beavers

North American Beaver

- Weighs 33 to 77 pounds (15 to 35 kilograms)
- Largest rodent in North America

Eurasian Beaver

- Weighs 40 to 64 pounds (18 to 29 kg)
- Largest rodent in Europe

Beaver History

Beavers have been on Earth for millions of years. Giant beavers, measuring up to 7 feet (2 meters) tall, lived in North America at the time of the last Ice Age. Fossils have been found that date back 1.4 million years. These beavers used their huge teeth to chop down trees and build dams.

When Europeans first came to North America, there were as many as 400 million beavers. The beaver was hunted for its thick fur, which was used to make coats and hats. Beaver **pelt** coats became so popular in Europe that the beaver was hunted almost to **extinction**.

Beavers are known to be a **keystone species**. As a keystone species, the U.S. government has protected the beaver. Today, there are millions of these animals in North America.

In the past, a trader could buy a beaver pelt in North America and sell it for 20 times the amount in Europe.

American Indians stretched and dried beaver skins on a hoop made from tree branches.

Beaver Shelter

Beavers live in lodges that they build in or near their dams. Lodges are large, strong, dome-shaped structures. They offer shelter from cold weather. Lodges also protect beavers from **predators**, such as wolves, otters, and foxes.

Many lodges have one chamber, or room. Some have a front chamber for eating and another room toward the back for sleeping. There is a small hole at the top of the lodge. It allows fresh air to enter so that the beavers can breathe. The floor is slightly above water level. This keeps it dry inside. The only way into the lodge is from the water.

When a dam floods an area, beavers begin building a lodge in the new lake or pond that forms. Beavers use tree trunks, branches, and mud to build the lodge. Each family of beavers builds its own dam, pond, and lodge.

Fascinating Facts

Beavers have been known to live in burrows, which they dig in the ground close to the water.

The flooded area around dams makes homes for other mammals, birds, fish, and insects.

Beaver Features

Beavers spend most of their lives in and around water. For this reason, their bodies have **adapted** to life in the water. Beaver have flaps of skin called webs between the toes of their hind feet. This helps them swim better. Beavers have a layer of fat under their skin and a thick coat of fur. The fur and fat keep beavers warm in freezing cold water.

FUR
A beaver's fur has two layers to help keep the animal warm. Beavers take an oily substance from **glands** under their tail and rub it all over their fur. This helps keep the fur clean, as well as waterproof.

TAIL
Beavers are known for their wide, flat tail. A beaver's tail can be 11.8 inches (30 cm) long and 7.1 inches (18 cm) wide. The beaver uses its tail on land for balance when carrying large sticks and branches. In the water, the tail is used for swimming. Beavers will slap their tail against the surface of the water to scare away predators or to warn the colony of trouble.

EYES

Beavers have clear eyelids that close over their eyes when they are underwater. This helps beavers see underwater and keeps water out of their eyes.

TEETH

Beavers have two long, sharp front teeth called **incisors**. These teeth are always growing. They can grow as much as 4 feet (1 m) every year. Chewing tree bark helps keep the teeth from growing too long. This also keeps their teeth sharp. Beavers' front teeth are covered with a hard, orange coating. This protects them from damage.

FEET

The beaver's hind feet are webbed. This helps the beaver push through the water when it swims. The hind feet have five toes, each with a rounded claw. The second toe on the hind foot is double-clawed. Beavers use this toe to groom their fur. The beaver's front paws are used to carry sticks, stones, and mud. The front feet have long, sharp claws that are used for digging.

What Do Beavers Eat?

Beavers are herbivores. This means they eat only plants. One of the beaver's main foods is cambium. This is a soft **tissue** near the top layer of wood. Beavers use their sharp teeth and claws to rip bark off tree trunks and branches to get to the cambium.

During the winter, it is difficult for beavers to move on land that is covered in snow. A colony will store sticks and branches near the entrance to the lodge. This stored food will keep the beaver colony fed throughout the long winter.

Beavers eat plants as well as wood. They swim to the bottom of their ponds to dig up plant roots from the soil.

Beavers have a special stomach that is able to digest, or break down, wood.

In summer, beavers add water plants, leaves, grass, fruit, thistles, seeds, and roots to their diet.

Beaver Life Cycle

Beavers begin to mate at three years old. They remain with the same mate for life. Together, they build a family and colony.

Birth

Baby beavers are called kits. They are born in late spring, about four months after the mating season. Each **litter** of beavers can have between one and nine kits. Beaver kits are born covered with fur, with their eyes open. They can walk and swim as soon as they are born. A newborn beaver is about 15 inches (38 cm) long and weighs about 0.5 to 1.5 pounds (0.2 to 0.7 kg).

One Day to One Month

Most beaver kits stay in the lodge for the first month of their life. It is dangerous for the kits to leave the lodge. Sometimes, the lodge is threatened by a predator. The mother beaver will carry her young in her mouth to a safe place.

Mating season takes place from January to February. Baby beavers are born about 110 days later. Females can have only one litter each year.

One Month to Two Years

Beaver kits less than one year old spend their time eating, growing, and learning. One-year-old beavers begin helping their parents store food and repair the lodge and dam.

Adult

Beavers leave their parents' lodge when they are two years old. They travel to new areas, where they begin building their own colonies. At three years old, beavers are ready to mate and begin a family of their own. Beavers can live to be about 20 years of age.

Encountering Beavers

In North America, beavers are quite common. They often share their **habitat** with humans. However, beavers are shy animals that are most active at night. They are rarely seen by people.

People may see beavers while hiking or camping at night in wooded places that are near water. It is important to never get too close to a beaver. Beavers may try to protect themselves if they feel threatened. Their sharp teeth and claws can be a danger.

Many people do not want beavers living in their neighborhood. Beavers damage trees, and dams can cause roads, yards, and fields to flood. It is a good idea to let a fish and wildlife officer know if there is a beaver living nearby. The officer can find a safe way to address the concern.

Fascinating Facts

In southeastern states, damage to crops, property, and roads from beavers costs more than $5 million a year.

When food is hard to find,
beavers move to a new home.

Myths and Legends

Beavers are an important animal in many American Indian legends. The beaver is known as a smart, hard working, and proud animal. Due to the beaver's excellent building abilities, some American Indian groups believe that the beaver helped the Great Spirit build Earth.

Early explorers in North America saw large beaver lodges and heard American Indian stories of these rodents. When the explorers returned to Europe, they told their own tales about beaver colonies and beavers' great skills as builders. Some people believed beavers used special tools and had a system of government. They were said to be nearly as smart as humans.

Beavers are seen in American Indian artwork, such as totem poles.

The Beaver's Tail

This is a Shoshone Indian legend about how the beaver got its flat tail.

A long time ago, Beaver and Otter lived near each other on the same river. One day, Otter built a slide, which he used to have fun. Beaver swam by on his way to cut down trees to fix his lodge. Otter laughed and asked Beaver why he always worked so hard. Beaver told Otter that he had fun early in the spring. With winter coming, Beaver had to fix his lodge and dam.

Otter challenged Beaver to build a slide. Beaver took great pride in his building skills. He told Otter that he could build a bigger slide than Otter had ever seen. Beaver walked up the side of the mountain and slid down on his backside. The rocks on the mountain hurt beaver. The next time he slid, he sat on his big tail. It worked very well. Beaver slid down the hill many more times. After, Beaver noticed Otter laughing at him. The sliding had flattened beaver's tail and rubbed off all the hair.

Frequently Asked Questions

Do beavers make sounds?

Answer: Beavers make whining, hissing, grunting, and snuffling sounds. Sounds are an important part of playing and grooming. They also show when a beaver is upset. Beaver kits whine more often than adults. They often whine when they need help from their parents.

What is the difference between a beaver and a muskrat?

Answer: Beavers are much larger than muskrats. A muskrat is like a type of large field mouse that lives in and around water. A muskrat's hind feet are not webbed, and the animal has a long, rat-like tail.

What do beaver tracks look like?

Answer: A beaver's tracks will show small front feet, with five toes and claws. The hind feet are much larger, and are webbed. A beaver trail will sometimes show the tail as well. This is because the tail drags behind the beaver as it walks.

Words to Know

adapted: changed over time to survive

dams: stick structures that hold back water

extinction: when there are no more of a species left in the world

glands: body organs that produce chemicals that help a human or animal stay healthy

habitat: the place where an animal lives

incisors: the long, sharp teeth at the front of a beaver's mouth

keystone species: animals on which all other nearby animals depend for survival

litter: a group of baby animals born together

mammals: warm-blooded, live-born animals that have a spine, fur, or hair, and drink milk from their mother

pelt: an animal's skin and fur

predators: animals that hunt other animals for food

rodent: a group of mammals that includes rats, mice, beavers, and rabbits; known for growing sharp front teeth for gnawing

species: a group of similar animals that can mate together

tissue: a group of cells in an animal or plant that have the same function

Index

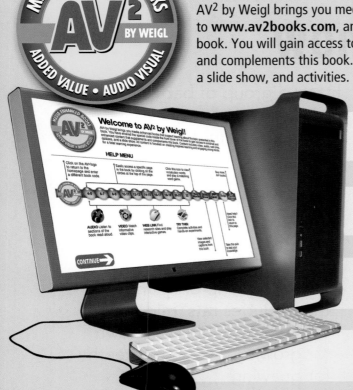

Log on to www.av2books.com

AV[2] by Weigl brings you media enhanced books that support active learning. Go to **www.av2books.com**, and enter the special code inside the front cover of this book. You will gain access to enriched and enhanced content that supplements and complements this book. Content includes video, audio, web links, quizzes, a slide show, and activities.

Audio
Listen to sections of
the book read aloud.

Video
Watch informative video clips.

Web Link
Find research sites and
play interactive games.

Try This!
Complete activities and
hands-on experiments.

WHAT'S ONLINE?

Try This! Complete activities and hands-on experiments.	**Web Link** Find research sites and play interactive games.	**Video** Watch informative video clips.	**EXTRA FEATURES**
Pages 6-7 Outline the differences between North American beavers and Eurasian beavers.	**Pages 6-7** Learn more about the Eurasian beaver.	**Pages 4-5** Watch a video about beavers living in nature.	 **Audio** Hear introductory au at the top of every p
Pages 12-13 List the five key features of the beaver.	**Pages 8-9** Find out how beavers can benefit humans.	**Pages 10-11** See how beavers build a lodge.	**Key Words** Study vocabulary, and play a matching word game.
Pages 16-17 Compare the similarities and differences between a beaver kit and an adult beaver.	**Pages 10-11** Play an interactive beaver game.	**Pages 14-15** Watch a beaver eating.	**Slide Show** View images and captions, and try a writing activity.
Page 22 Test your beaver knowledge.	**Pages 18-19** Find out fascinating facts about beavers.		**AV[2] Quiz** Take this quiz to test your knowledge
	Pages 20-21 Read more stories about beavers.		

Due to the dynamic nature of the Internet, some of the URLs and activities provided as part of AV[2] by Weigl may hav changed or ceased to exist. AV[2] by Weigl accepts no responsibility for any such changes. All media enhanced books regularly monitored to update addresses and sites in a timely manner. Contact AV[2] by Weigl at 1-866-649-3445 or av2books@weigl.com with any questions, comments, or feedback.